MW00630360

In The Shadow of Your Wings

© Copyright 2006 Master Press
by Sue Wesley Sewell

Published by Master Press

318 S.E. 4th Terrace

Cape Coral, Florida 33990

Distributed by Master Press
In The Shadow of Your Wings Sue Wesley Sewell
ISBN 0-9759049-8-1

Visit our website at: www.master-press.com
800-325-9136 or 239-772-0634

About the cover and artist, Daniel Gerhartz

In the December, following my final chemo treatment, and a couple of weeks after my second reconstruction surgery, my husband and I were wandering around enjoying the gorgeous weather and viewing the art in Scottsdale, Arizona. There are many great galleries in Old Town and we came across the painting that graces the cover of this book. Instantly I was struck with intense emotions. This painting was me. How could the artist have known what I had experienced?

I began to inquire about the artist and the subject matter. I was told that the title was "In the Shadow of Your Wings." That sounded scriptural to me. As I questioned the salesperson, they volunteered to call the artist in Wisconsin and inquire about the history for me. Mr. Gerhartz confirmed that the painting was based on: "Keep me as the apple of the eye; hide me in the shadow of Your wings'" (Psalm 17:8, NASB). This painting touched my husband and me in a powerful way. The total peace that the subject in the painting was experiencing was so vibrant. Needless to say, we walked out of the gallery with the painting. It now hangs in our entry, where we are reminded daily of God's grace and peace.

In late January 2004, the Lord directed me to share my experience in a book to encourage those who are faced with the diagnosis of breast cancer and an unknown future. As I approached completion of the book, I phoned the artist again and asked for his permission to use it as the cover of my devotional book. I shared with him my recent history and how well he had captured my own emotions with the woman serenely curled up in the shadow of the wing of God. He generously granted my request. I hope that through the readings, you too will find peace for the journey ahead of you.

Sue Sewell

February 2006

This book is dedicated to my friend, valiant prayer warrior, breast cancer patient and trusted sister in Christ ~ Karen Kelly Keating.

Christ as Your Personal Savior

It may be that a friend has given you this book as an encouragement or you may have bought it out of curiosity. Either way, you are now reading through it. Maybe you don't really understand what it means to have a personal relationship with Jesus Christ. All the experiences and trust I refer to, in these pages, requires that knowledge.

Although God's Word is written to everyone, the promises are for His children. For you to lay claim to His promises, you must kneel before God and confess you are a sinner with no hope, except for the gift of the blood of Jesus Christ. God desires a relationship with you, but because of Adam's and Eve's rebellion in the Garden of Eden, man fell into sin and became eternally separated from God because of that sin. In His desire to regain that fellowship and save mankind from eternal separation and hell, God the Father sent His Son, through the power of the Holy Spirit, to be conceived by a virgin. The virgin, named Mary, named her son Jesus, as God commanded. With the help of her husband, Joseph, she raised Him in their home in Nazareth. At the appointed time, Jesus left His earthly parents and began the ministry that God the Father had sent Him to do. For three years he gathered disciples and traveled throughout the Holy Land performing miracles, healing the sick and teaching the Word of God. Although He was fully man, He never committed sin. Often tempted by Satan to reject heaven and accept Satan's temporal gifts, Jesus knew the Old Testament and was able to escape the power of temptation. He suffered rejection, abuse, and loss of friends and loved ones, but never lost sight of His purpose on earth. He came to save mankind from eternal separation from the Father. To do this God demanded a blood sacrifice. The blood God required had to be from a spotless "lamb." Christ was the only perfect man to ever live, and it was His blood that had to be shed for our salvation. He did this willingly to bring you and me home with Him for eternity. It was a gift, pure and simple. There is nothing you can do to earn it; it must simply be received.

Christ told His disciples that He would rise again on the third day after He was crucified. Just as He promised, He arose and appeared to over 500 people. History records all these events.

Now it's your turn. If you are ready, kneel to receive God's free gift, and pray the following prayer:

Father,

I confess I am a sinner. I can do nothing to change my sin nature and earn my salvation. I believe that Your perfect Son, Jesus, was born of a virgin, crucified on a cross, and was raised on the third day with a new immortal body. He paid the debt I could not pay and I accept Him as my Savior. I want to know Your Word and claim your promises for myself. Amen.

God tells us in John 3:16–17, "For God so loved the world that he gave his only Son, so that everyone who believes in him will not perish but have eternal life. God did not send his Son into the world to condemn it, but to save it" (NLT).

God has chosen you, but the question remains – will you choose Him? I sincerely pray that you will!

In the Shadow of Your Wings

Devotionals to Encourage
Breast Cancer Patients

by
Sue Wesley Sewell

In the Shadow of Your Wings

Table of Contents

Christ as Your Personal Savior

Foreward

Somehow we forget that life really is fragile, and that radical destabilizing news is only a phone call away. Like the call from your doctor telling you that the tests don't look good. How unsettling to hear that without you knowing about it, down deep inside, cells have been massing themselves against your body. That if not checked life as you've known it may be a thing of the past. Or worse yet, the cancer is accelerated, and immediate steps must be taken to try to save your life.

Where do you go for peace and comfort in the midst of the turmoil that that kind of news brings to your soul? If you have cultivated a growing relationship with God, great solace is found in His presence, love, mercy, and grace. How good to know that this is the short, often nasty world and that because of Jesus, the better world is still ahead. But even with those thoughts tucked deeply in our hearts we foften need to feel that we are not alone...that others have gone through these waters before...that in their stories we can find hope and confidence to face our own journey with strength.

Knowing that in suffering we need to hear from co-strugglers, I encouraged Sue and Doug to follow their desire to tell others their story by writing this booklet. Martie and I watched them go through the deep waters of cancer and admired their honesty, candor, and confidence in the face of dismal and devastating circumstances. Needless to say, I am delighted to see their story in print.

These pages are not penned by professionals who make a living off of writing about other people's problems. Nor is it laced with pious platitudes that have a nice ring about them, but in the face of reality have no weight to help us when the chips are down. We don't need any more books like that.

This is real stuff about real struggles shared with unusual and helpful transparency. They have chosen to let us in to the inner sanctuary of their struggle. But that doesn't surprise me...Doug and Sue are that kind of people.

If you are facing what they have faced, you will find help and encouragement here. You will know that you are not alone!

Dr. Joe Stowell

Heavenly

In these four things I am

Father,

    I was designed by Your hand,

confident ~

      Saved by Your Son,

        Filled with Your Spirit,

    And ~ I am walking in the circumstances

        Of Your sovereign will.

      Give me the courage, strength, and

grace to

        Glorify You in all that I say

and do . . .

sue sewell

Shocked by Reality

Lord, today I found out that I have breast cancer. This can't be right. This morning I was healthy. This afternoon I'm facing a life-threatening, insidious monster. They use words I don't understand. What is CDIS? What are "calcifications"? What does invasive or inflammatory mean? Is there a dictionary for this? Where do I turn? How do I know whom to trust? What about my family? I have responsibilities I have to take care of! It can't be true! They must have made a mistake. I am afraid. Where do I start? This is more than I can process. This can't be happening!

This is where we all start, but having walked this path I can encourage you. You have an opportunity to know the Lord far more intimately than ever before. You have a chance to experience His grace beyond measure. From now on when you think of the "Big C word," think CHRIST. Christ alone.

First, tell your family. Next, call a friend. You need someone on the outside to walk with you. Your family is scared, too. Get the word out to all your family and friends that you are going to need their prayerful support. Ask them to pray that you can find healing, peace, and comfort. You are probably used to being the one whom others depend on. Today that has changed. One of your first lessons is learning to lean on others. The power of the saints praying for you will empower you. When you lean on others, you are leaning on the Body of Christ. You will now see Christ in the flesh of your fellow believers.

The first friend I called asked if she could run interference for my husband and me with our other friends. She suggested that people call her about visits and bringing food so we would not be overwhelmed. I really hadn't considered whether I would be up to taking phone calls and visits from loving friends on a regular basis. The week I was in the hospital, along with the first couple of weeks at home, it was very helpful to have this insulation. I would call, or likely e-mail, the daily status report and let her coordinate schedules. Left to myself, I would have wanted to do and see more, when I really needed to convalesce.

People always want to help; you just have to know how to direct them. Enlist someone to act as a buffer for you, and allow the Lord to bless them by serving you.

These people will surround you, but their response will depend totally on you. If you are strong, they will be strong. If you need to cry, they will cry with you. Today is just the first day.

Your doctor has just discovered one of your most dreaded fears. It is very important to realize that this is not the worst day of your life. Quite possibly, it's the best. Without this discovery your cancer would have grown. But thankfully, you can take action.

Take His Word — grab it as though it were your only life preserver.

Journal

"If anyone gives you even a cup of water because you belong to the Messiah, I assure you, that person will be rewarded" (Mark 9:41, NLT).

"Have I not commanded you? Be strong and of good courage; be not frightened, neither be dismayed; for the Lord your God is with you wherever you go" (Joshua 1:9, RSV).

_____

_____

_____

_____

_____

_____

_____

_____

_____

_____

_____

_____

_____

_____

Paralyzed by Fear

Lord, I am so scared. There are things I really need to do, but all I can do is cry. I sit and stare straight ahead. If I don't say it out loud, then it's not true. But I have to make doctor appointments—possibly surgeons to remove my breast, plastic surgeons for reconstruction, MRI's, and scans of every kind. I am so overwhelmed.

Today I need to begin to take charge of my medical care. It is fortunate, in this day and age, that there are many places that deal strictly with "breast care" in the larger metropolitan areas of the United States. If you live in a rural area, you may be dependent on your local physician to refer you to a larger facility. You are entering "Breast Care 101." The internet is a great resource, but it can be too much to take in all at once. Don't try to read it all. Find a couple of sites, such as Breast Cancer Online (bco.org) or Breast Cancer Org. (breastcancer.org). The Susan G. Komen Foundation (komen.org) is also a great resource, as well as breastdiseases.com and laf.org.

Doctors will give you pamphlets with some of the buzzwords that you will become accustomed to hearing and using. Begin now to realize how very grateful you are to our Lord and Savior, that in His boundless wisdom, He created medical science that can address many of the medical issues of the 21st century. Ask your friends to pray that you will have wisdom and discernment. And strength! Always strength! Going through the routine is a very wearying process.

Learn to focus on God's Word. Store it in your heart.

Journal

"When I think of the wisdom and scope of God's plan, I fall to my knees and pray to the Father, the Creator of everything in heaven and on earth. I pray that from his glorious, unlimited resources he will give you mighty inner strength through his Holy Spirit. And I pray that Christ will be more and more at home in your hearts as you trust in him. May your roots go down deep into the soil of God's marvelous love. And may you have the power to understand, as all God's people should, how wide, how long, how high, and how deep his love really is. May you experience the love of Christ, though it is so great you will never fully understand it. Then you will be filled with the fullness of life and power that comes from God" (Ephesians 3:14–19, NLT).

_____

_____

_____

_____

_____

_____

_____

_____

_____

_____

_____

It's Cancer

It's beginning to settle into my head now. They say I have cancer. I don't feel sick. I don't look sick. But, apparently, I am sick. I am now beginning to wage war on an enemy that I cannot see. It is a ravaging enemy, and I will remember at all times that <u>I am at war</u>. I can cry, but I must remember this is an enemy that will take no prisoners. if given the option. I must gather up all the ammunition I can carry and fight with zeal. I know that all of my tomorrows have changed because of this enemy. That doesn't mean I have no tomorrows, only that they will be different. I am now a part of a new sorority/fraternity. I have a common bond with others who have gone before me, and those who will come behind me. If I forget I'm at war, I will be tempted to surrender to fear. Satan finds his greatest strength is planting the seed of fear in my heart.

I begin, today, practicing putting Christ in control of my every thought. In Christ I have hope, not fear. I am walking hand in hand with my Lord down a difficult path. I walk with Him because I know I can trust Him. I know that He will not reject or neglect me. I know that He alone has the strength I need to face the unknown circumstances of tomorrow. He alone will reach down, gently put His arms around me, and pick me up. He will carry me when I can walk no more.

My emotions overcome me with dread of the unknown. They roll over me like the swells of the rising tide. I remind myself that there is no sin in my emotions. This is the way God has made me. When I feel sad and despairing, I remind myself that what I know is more important than how I feel. I call on the Scriptures I have hidden in my heart. My emotions are totally unpredictable, changing without warning. But what I know is God is immutable—never changing; the same yesterday, today, and tomorrow. In Him alone can I trust.

Journal

"And those who know Your name will put their trust in You; for You, Lord, have not forsaken those who seek You" (Psalm 9:10, NKJV).

"Don't copy the behavior and customs of this world, but let God transform you into a new person by changing the way you think. Then you will know what God wants you to do, and you will know how good and pleasing and perfect his will really is" (Romans 12:2, NLT).

_____

_____

_____

_____

_____

_____

_____

_____

_____

_____

_____

_____

_____

_____

Journaling

There may be people in your life that you watch; they have a glow about them whenever you see them. There is something about them that is different. You can't put your finger on it, but it's there. Oswald Chambers reminds us in his book, *My Utmost for His Highest* (April 14), "'The joy of the Lord is your strength.' Where do the saints get their joy from? If we did not know some saints, we would say, 'Oh, he, or she, has nothing to bear.' Lift the veil. The fact that the peace and the light and the joy of God are there is proof that the burden is there too."

My heart desired that joy. I began to sit alone with the Lord and journal. Friends and loved ones shared Scripture with me. I saw Scripture I'd known for years with new eyes and a new heart. God's Word is a great comfort. As fear of the future crept in, I was reminded that the only fear I had room for was,

> *"The fear of the LORD is the beginning of knowledge. . ."*
> *(Proverbs 1:7a, NKJV)*

and

> *"This is what he says to all humanity: 'The fear of the Lord is true wisdom; to forsake evil is real understanding'" (Job 28:28, NLT).*

With that knowledge in my heart, I began to realize I was wasting my emotional energy fearing cancer. With His Word once again stored in my heart, I came to a place of total peace and serenity.

With this peace comes a new depth of joy for each day, a greater hunger for God's Word and His presence, and less fear of surgery, follow-up treatment, and facing an unknown future. I turned to my journal and found a private place where I could call out to the Lord. I learned to let His spirit flow through me and fill my heart and mind. His presence simply enveloped me. I began to see that there was going to be a blessing in having cancer. The intimacy with God surprised me.

Journaling

C. S. Lewis wrote a book titled *Surprised by Joy*. It describes my experience. Because I had found peace in my circumstances, my opportunity for ministry was now expanded to caregivers, family, friends, and others standing on the sidelines watching.

I have spent a lifetime telling the Lord I wanted my life to be a testimony for Him. I don't think I had recognized that a testimony is drawn from a personal experience of total dependence on God. And total dependence does not come easily.

Journal

"Be strong, and let your heart take courage, all you who wait for the LORD!" (Psalm 31:24, RSV).

"Be strong and of good courage, do not fear nor be afraid of them; for the LORD your God, He is the One who goes with you. He will not leave you nor forsake you" (Deuteronomy 31:6, NKJV).

_____

_____

_____

_____

_____

_____

_____

_____

_____

_____

_____

_____

_____

_____

Facing Reality

Today I remind myself, once more, that I have cancer. I must learn to do this without being overwhelmed with fear and questions of "Why me?" The real question is, "Why *not* me?" Is there something so special about me that I should be spared suffering when Christ was not spared? Today I will surrender my cancer to God, just as Christ surrendered in *Luke 22:42 (NLT):*

> *"Father, if you are willing, please take this cup of suffering away from me. Yet I want your will, not mine."*

Have you heard God's voice? Have you cleared your mind of the "busyness" of your world and the fear of the unknown long enough to hear the sweet words of Jesus? Can you look to the Lord with a heart of gratitude? Can you say, "Thank You Jesus for the opportunity to be totally dependent on You for my health, treatment and recovery. Thank You for my salvation and the promise of eternity in heaven with You"? Have you made Christ Lord of your life? There will be no peace until that is done.

Last week you thought you were in control of your life. You made plans and executed them. Facing cancer was not on your list. Today it *is* your list. There is nothing that takes priority, yet life continues to spin around you. Jobs must be completed, meals have to be prepared, errands have to be run, laundry piles up in the hamper, and phone calls need to be returned. All that was before "**is**". Now cancer and doctor appointments have restructured your day. You are now much more aware of the sovereignty of God than ever before. He placed the stars in the heavens; He drew the boundaries of the tide in the sand; He separated daylight from darkness; He carved the depth of the Grand Canyon, and He knew you before the beginning of time.

This may be one of the biggest lessons you will ever learn as a disciple of Christ. He *is* in control. Can you digest this information? Can you acknowledge that a loving, gracious, and just God would allow you to be trusted with such a burden as cancer?

Journal

"We can make our plans, but the LORD determines our steps" (Proverbs 16:9, NLT).

"For by grace you have been saved through faith, and that not of yourselves; it is the gift of God, not of works, lets anyone should boast. For we are His workmanship, created in Christ Jesus for good works, which God prepared beforehand that we should walk in them" (Ephesians 2:8-10, NKJV).

_____

_____

_____

_____

_____

_____

_____

_____

_____

_____

_____

_____

_____

Power of an Army

Have you taken the opportunity to enlist your army of prayer warriors to storm the gates of heaven on your behalf? Does this sound a little selfish to you? Do you want to keep the cancer quiet? Do you intend to win this battle—spiritually, physically, and emotionally? If so, you will need an army!

At one point a treasured godly friend asked me if he could tell others so they could pray for both my husband and me as we walked the unknown path that lay ahead. My first response was, "No. Thank you, though." As I walked away from that conversation, I wondered why I was unwilling to tell others. Faced with my own response, I discovered a couple of things. First, telling made it more real. Second, I was afraid I would have to explain every detail, and, basically, I didn't want to talk about it.

After thinking about it overnight, I went back to my friend and gave him permission. I was emotionally unprepared for the loving encouragement I received. My own fear, selfishness, privacy, pride, whatever, almost robbed me of the indescribable joy and power that came from the prayers of Christian warriors. Many of the people put me on the prayer list of their Sunday school or their Bible study group. I'm sure there were numerous people praying for me that I will never know about. My willingness to allow others to know of my situation transformed me. Without a doubt, my relationship with Christ changed. There were many days when I couldn't pray for myself, but others empowered me as they prayed on my behalf. I began to send e-mails to my "prayer warriors" on a regular basis. Many of the prayer warriors lived long distances from us, but e-mail allowed me to give them frequent updates. On some occasions, I made special requests. It also allowed me to ask them how I could pray for them. I must confess I selfishly gained more through this than through any other source.

Journal

"And the Holy Spirit helps us in our distress. For we don't even know what we should pray for, nor how we should pray. But the Holy Spirit prays for us with groanings that cannot be expressed in words. And the Father who knows all hearts knows what the Spirit is saying, for the Spirit pleads for us believers in harmony with God's own will" (Romans 8:26–27, NLT).

"And so, dear brothers and sisters, we can boldly enter heaven's Most Holy Place because of the blood of Jesus" (Hebrews 10:19, NLT).

_____

_____

_____

_____

_____

_____

_____

_____

_____

_____

_____

_____

_____

Gifts in the Darkness

What gift has the Lord given you in the midst of this trial that you have not thanked Him for? For me, it was support of old friends and new. My husband was out of the country the day I was diagnosed. I called a sister in Christ and she became glued to my hip. She insisted on going with me to the surgeon, the reconstruction surgeon, and the MRI the next day. She asked many questions. I asked few. She remembered the answers to all, and I barely remember being there.

We had planned a trip months before the diagnosis, and I asked the doctors if I could still go. They assured me that I could, and should, go and enjoy myself. I found out on Tuesday I had cancer and left for our trip on Friday. I really had not had time to even begin to process the diagnosis, much less think of intelligent questions. As my husband and I boarded our plane I turned to him and said, "I wonder who God will have for me on this trip?" When we arrived at our destination and met the other guests from all over the U.S., I discovered God had brought a surgeon and a gynecologist on our trip. The surgeon was from Mississippi, the gynecologist was from Illinois, and we were from Texas. It's funny, but I really wasn't surprised at the encounter. I simply rejoiced.

The surgeon became my confidant. He listened to my questions and answered questions I didn't know I had. He was the first to tell me that I would be living with cancer the rest of my life. That was a real shock. I was of the mind that if you survived five years, you were cured. Not so in today's medical world. It is considered dormant, but it can always raise its ugly head and surprise me in the future. He spent time with my husband telling him what to expect. He continued to walk with us for the next four months. We had planned our trip in October the previous year. I was diagnosed in May. The following June I met the people God had placed in my path months before. Both of these physicians were little pearls that God gave me to remind me that He knew where I was and what I needed.

Though the journey is hard and frightening, God will lay pearls in your path. Look for them, expect them and thank God for them.

Journal

"'For I know the plans I have for you,' says the Lord. 'They are plans for good and not for disaster, to give you a future and a hope. In those days when you pray, I will listen. If you look for me in earnest, you will find me when you seek me. I will be found by you,' says the Lord. 'I will end your captivity and restore your fortunes . . .'" (Jeremiah 29:11–14a, NLT).

_____

_____

_____

_____

_____

_____

_____

_____

_____

_____

_____

_____

_____

_____

Knowing Jesus

What does it mean to *know* Jesus? Does it mean that you know He is God's one and only Son because you heard it in Sunday school? Maybe your parents told you about Jesus, or perhaps a roommate in college. If you've only heard about Him, you may not know Him at all. One way you can really know Jesus is through His Word. God wants to be known. He sent Jesus so that we might see God and His attributes in the flesh. He left us His Word so that we might know Him. He equipped believers with the Holy Spirit so that we might be directly linked to God the Father and Jesus the Son. Once you become a believer you are one of His children.

If you do not know Jesus as your Savior and Lord, now is the perfect time to face God through prayer, confess you are a sinner and unable to save yourself. In that moment, acknowledge that Christ's crucifixion on the cross was the price you could not pay for your salvation and accept Him as your Savior.

> *"For God so loved the world that He gave His only begotten Son, that whosoever believes in Him should not perish but have everlasting life. For God did not send His Son into the world to condemn the world, but that the world through Him might be saved" (John 3:16–17, NKJV).*

As you make Him Lord of your life and your circumstance, you need to know about His character. Is He annoyed when we are weak in flesh or in spirit? Is He always just and fair? Does He punish His children with sickness and death? What you need to understand is Christ became flesh, so that we might know the Father. He tells us,

> *"He who has seen me has seen the Father; how can you say, 'Show us the Father'? Do you not believe that I am in the Father and the Father in me? The words that I say to you I do not speak on my own authority; but the Father who dwells in me does his works" (John 14:9b–10, RSV).*

You are in a difficult place. Your spirit may know that God is trustworthy, but your emotions may stumble. You must be confident that you are not being punished! You may never know why an innocent child dies or a missionary is killed in service to the Lord. I doubt that you will ever know why you have cancer and your friend, who is genetically predisposed, doesn't. You can know that our heavenly Father is sovereign. ("Sovereign" is a big word that tells us that *nothing* comes our way without God's permission.) He is never surprised by our circumstance. He knows what purpose He has designed for each of our lives, and He allows the circumstances in our lives to perfect us - to conform us to the image of Christ.

Journal

"And we know that God causes everything to work together for the good of those who love God and are called according to his purpose for them. For God knew his people in advance, and he chose them to become like his Son, so that his Son would be the firstborn, with many brothers and sisters" (Romans 8:28–29, NLT).

As you walk daily, carrying the heaviness of confusion, remember that Christ even made provision for your burden.

"Then Jesus said, 'Come to me, all of you who are weary and carry heavy burdens, and I will give you rest. Take my yoke upon you. Let me teach you, because I am humble and gentle, and you will find rest for your souls. For my yoke fits perfectly, and the burden I give you is light'" (Matthew 11: 28–30, NLT).

_____

_____

_____

_____

_____

_____

_____

_____

_____

_____

Sadness

Some days are better than others. Then there are shadowy moments when I find myself slipping into sadness. Not so much fear, but sadness. I can't tell you why I stumble. Without warning I am gripped with sorrow as my companion. At these times I tend to want to sneak off by myself, curl up with a soft down pillow and a warm snuggly blanket, and just pull the covers up over my head. I don't want to be a burden to anyone. I don't want them worrying about me. I need a touch from Jesus in the flesh. This is the time I must call on a Christian brother/sister. They must be one I can trust, one who won't despair for me, one who won't judge me or question my faith, and one who knows my faith and understands my needs. I need one who will quietly listen to me if I feel like talking, but most of all, one who will let me work through my emotions.

Good-meaning friends and family can squash me today. I am very vulnerable, and very raw. Sometimes I don't think I can trust anyone with this because I fear they will think I don't trust the Lord. I do trust Him, but I am weak and today I am struggling. Too many people are watching . . . I don't want to fail God, but I am so weary.

I pray carefully, asking for the right person. I know that the wrong person can drain me of what little emotional strength I have left. Praying and journaling brings back some of my spiritual strength. He alone knows the desires of my heart, and He alone can meet them. He gives me a sister to confide in, one who has walked this road and knows better than I the experience of the emotional and physical fatigue I encounter. She listens quietly and loves me unconditionally. Now I have seen the body of Christ at work, and I am touched by His "hand." I will know how to touch someone in the future.

Journal

"Just as our bodies have many parts and each part has a special function, so it is with Christ's body. We are all parts of his one body, and each of us has different work to do. And since we are all one body in Christ, we belong to each other, and each of us needs all the others. . . . When others are happy, be happy with them. If they are sad, share their sorrow" *(Romans 12:4–5, 15, NLT).*

"He heals the brokenhearted, binding up their wounds. . . . How great is our Lord! His power is absolute! His understanding is beyond comprehension!" *(Psalm 147:3, 5, NLT).*

Humility

In the midst of my ordeal, we took a trip with a well-known bible teacher, and then president of Moody Bible Institute, Dr. Joe Stowell. One evening he spoke to us about the church of Laodicea, in Revelation. He taught us that their primary sin was their sin of "independence." They didn't need anyone, especially God. Well I knew I needed God, but what I began to realize was that I was going to need others. I saw my sin of "**pride**" in big black bold letters. I would need someone to drive me, to cook and clean, someone to reach up to the shelf, to wash my hair, to change my bandages, and apply medicine. I liked being the caregiver. I was a mother, and I knew how to give. The double mastectomy and chemotherapy I was facing would change my role, at least temporarily. Now I was going to have to learn how to receive.

The shell of my exterior was beginning to crack wide open. I had to let others serve me. At that point, I began to praise God that He had revealed to me what a huge sin self-sufficiency was in my life. I never wanted to hear Him say to me that He would "spew me out of His mouth" as He had said to the Laodiceans.

As the Lord walks with you on this pilgrimage, ask Him to open your eyes and your heart so that you will recognize your needs, and allow Him to provide for them. This is a precious time for your loved ones and friends to do something for you. They will become the "hands of Christ."

Recognize that the Lord wants to teach others through their service to you. Everyone who is a part of your life will have an opportunity to know God more intimately as He uses them. Pray that you will humble yourself and look to Him to meet your needs. Ask for a gentle, gracious, and receptive spirit. You will see the body of Christ as you have never seen it before. As you humble yourself, you will praise Him for the miraculous ways He will provide.

Journal

"Unseal my lips, O Lord, that I may praise you. You would not be pleased with sacrifices, or I would bring them. If I brought you a burnt offering, you would not accept it. The sacrifice you want is a broken spirit. A broken and repentant heart, O God, you will not despise" (Psalm 51:15–17, NLT).

"The high and lofty one who inhabits eternity, the Holy One, says this: 'I live in that high and holy place with those whose spirits are contrite and humble. I refresh the humble and give new courage to those with repentant hearts'" (Isaiah 57:15, NLT).

"This is what the LORD says: 'Heaven is my throne, and the earth is my footstool. Could you ever build me a temple as good as that? Could you build a dwelling place for me? Hands have made both heaven and earth, and they are mine. I, the LORD, have spoken!' I will bless those who have humble and contrite hearts, who tremble at my word" (Isaiah 66:1–2, NLT).

_____

_____

_____

_____

_____

_____

_____

_____

Cancer Plus Family Can Equal Stress

Outside of the cancer, dealing with family is one of the most difficult pressures we may face. Our family comes to our rescue, wanting more than anything to comfort us and carry some of the burden. Their motives and desires are pure. They are helpless and they are afraid for us. This puts us in a conundrum. We see their stress and feel a responsibility to help ease their burden. We sense that we must keep a "happy face", disguising whatever may be going on inside to protect those we love. Now we are carrying our own fear *and* the concerns of those who love us. We want them around, yet we feel guilty for the additional emotional weight they bring. When this happens, we feel backed into a corner and want to escape. This desire to flee can bring immense guilt, and saddled with the unknown we are already facing, can lead to despair. What a heavy burden! How do we tell them that we love them, but their emotions are making our struggle more difficult?

The truth is the best tool, but phrasing the truth delicately, so that it is not hurtful, requires thought and skill. Spend time in prayer and Scripture, equipping yourself for the conversation. Try something like, "I see your concern for me and I am so very grateful for your willingness to help me. Right now, all I can do is face my own fears and emotions. If I am short with you, please forgive me. I need space to process the battle ahead. Thank you for being there. Please know that I will call on you when I need you, but for today, this moment, I need some space." You cannot be responsible for their response; you can only let them know your needs. They will have to work through their own feelings. Try not to become defensive, using "you" statements. It will only bring more stress.

When this stress is added to the anxiety we are already facing, it is a formula for serious depression. The doctors recognize this. Discuss your emotional situation with your doctors. If they recommend antidepressants, don't hesitate to consider this as an option. It is not a reflection of spiritual weakness. We are comprised of many parts - intellect, emotions, and spirit. Our emotions have a mind of their own, neither good nor bad. Don't add guilt or a sense of spiritual failure as a further burden.

Journal

"We are pressed on every side by troubles, but we are not crushed and broken. We are perplexed, but we don't give up and quit. We are hunted down, but God never abandons us. We get knocked down, but we get up again and keep going" (2 Corinthians 4:8–9, NLT).

_____

_____

_____

_____

_____

_____

_____

_____

_____

_____

_____

_____

_____

_____

_____

_____

_____

_____

_____

_____

_____

Bad Days

Was yesterday a difficult day for you? Or maybe this morning? Some days moved along smoothly, and then out of nowhere, I would be flooded with fear, followed swiftly by tears. Not depression or despair, just salty, crocodile tears. The continuing fear of the unknown can be consuming. Facing radiation, surgery, or chemo, and maybe more surgery, or more chemo, without the guarantee that the cancer will never come back is overpowering. Please, Lord, NO!

Do my tears surprise or disappoint God? Was He expecting me to be spiritually and emotionally stronger? Was this whole diagnosis and treatment a trial God had designed, specifically, for me to prove my faith? Was I failing Him? People were watching, was I letting God down? Are you? Are you trying to prove that you are something that you can't be? Do you find this burden too big to bear? Basically, there are things we can know and things we can't. As Isaiah quotes the Lord:

> *"'For My thoughts are not your thoughts, nor are your ways My ways,'" says the Lord. 'For as the heavens are higher than the earth, so are My ways higher than your ways, and My thoughts than your thoughts'" (Isaiah 55:8-9, NKJV).*

We can know that God does not condemn us for our tears. David writes,

> *"You keep track of all my sorrows. You have collected all my tears in your bottle. You have recorded each one in your book" (Psalm 56:8, NLT).*

Is there a more tender picture than that of the God of creation seeing our pain and suffering and gathering our tears in a bottle? Be comforted by knowing that He does see you. When tears come, so does He!

Take time to equip yourself with God's promises so that you can call on them.

Journal

"I will never leave you or forsake you" (Hebrews 13:5b, NKJV).

"The Lord is close to the brokenhearted; he rescues those who are crushed in spirit" (Psalm 34:18, NLT).

Paul gives us all the instruction we need to conquer our fear:

"We are human, but we don't wage war with human plans and methods. We use God's mighty weapons, not mere worldly weapons, to knock down the Devil's strongholds" (2 Corinthians 10:3–4, NLT).

"Put on all of God's armor so that you will be able to stand firm against all strategies and tricks of the Devil. For we are not fighting against people made of flesh and blood, but against the evil rulers and authorities of the unseen world, against those mighty powers of darkness who rule this world, and against wicked spirits in the heavenly realms" (Ephesians 6:11–12, NLT).

_____

_____

_____

_____

_____

_____

_____

_____

_____

_____

_____

_____

The Decision

Sooner or later, the day arrives when final decisions are made and treatment begins. My husband and I consulted four physicians and chose the third most aggressive option offered. Although I had only been diagnosed with invasive breast cancer in my right breast, we chose to have a double mastectomy, followed by four rounds of AC chemotherapy and then five years of hormone-blocking drugs. My surgery took place five weeks after my original diagnosis.

But first, it's surgery. Surgery can be a very frightening thing. It requires total submission to a variety of physicians. We elected to have a surgical oncologist do the mastectomy, followed immediately by the plastic surgeon who would begin reconstruction. When we made this decision we had no idea that this would require over nine hours of anesthesia.

Where do I begin? Just as God had done for the previous five weeks, He met my spiritual needs in the surgery room with a beautiful Christian nurse from Africa. I'm sure she broke every protocol of the hospital, but she gathered my family, friends, and minister from the waiting room. With thirteen people present, she had the group circle me, join hands, and prayed the blood of Christ over me. Is there anything more one could ask for? As I lay there totally helpless, covered by a blanket, wearing a surgical gown, and dependent on God and the medical community, He met my needs and brought me perfect peace.

You may not have a Christian surgical nurse, but you will have family and friends. Take this opportunity to look to Christ for strength and peace. If possible, invite your nurse to join your family in the circle of the love of the body of Christ. Pray for protection, skilled hands, peace, encouragement, the presence of the Holy Spirit, and whatever you are led to plead. God rejoices in hearing your requests. It is His desire to meet your every need.

Journal

"The LORD is a shelter for the oppressed, a refuge in times of trouble. Those who know your name trust in you, for you, O LORD, have never abandoned anyone who searches for you" (Psalm 9:9–10, NLT).

"I wait quietly before God, for my hope is in him. He alone is my rock and my salvation, my fortress where I will not be shaken. My salvation and my honor come from God alone. He is my refuge, a rock where no enemy can reach me. O my people, trust in him at all times. Pour out your heart to him, for God is our refuge" (Psalm 62:5–8, NLT).

_____

_____

_____

_____

_____

_____

_____

_____

_____

_____

_____

_____

_____

_____

_____

The Surgery

What is it really like to wake up after surgery without breasts? I expected it to be very traumatic, not to mention painful. I wondered if this would be my downfall. As with everything, there is so much to be done and not much time to dwell on the negative.

There are decisions to make before the surgery regarding reconstruction. If you choose to have reconstruction, there are choices to make there as well. We chose reconstruction without much hesitation. Because of previous surgery repairing an abdominal hernia following the birth of my twins, I was faced with the option of a latissimus flap, or simply having expanders dropped in between the chest cavity and the remaining chest skin. We chose the flap. Be forewarned—this is not a solution for "sissies"! The surgery and recovery are longer. There are twice as many incisions, but it held the most promise for a more natural result long term. Your doctor will explain your options to you.

It was our desire to have as short of a hospital stay as possible. The surgery was lengthy, with the plastic surgeon immediately following the surgical oncologist, but it allowed both procedures to be done during one hospital stay.

God was very gracious to me. When I awoke, I found that the expanders already had 200cc of fluid creating small mounds on my chest. I think I would have been fine without them, but I was grateful that the Lord had seen my concern and gone before me with a solution.

Chemo began six weeks after the mastectomy and continued for three months. Periodically, during chemo, fluid was added to the expanders to enlarge the cavity, which the physician had created to support the implants. Four weeks following the final chemo, the second surgery was done to remove the expanders and insert the implants into the chest cavity. One more surgery was required to complete the process of reconstruction.

As the physicians are fighting the cancer and are attempting to create a new you, God is transforming your mind to create a new creature in Christ. They can never recreate what God created. There will be numbness, scars and soreness. In the flap surgery, some strength is lost in the shoulders, but it's insignificant. I would never be mistaken for "Cosmo girl", but my clothing does look natural and I feel comfortable in my own skin. These choices are very personal and should be made with much information, prayer, and discussion with your team of physicians and your family.

Journal

"Charm is deceptive, and beauty does not last; but a woman who fears the LORD will be greatly praised" (Proverbs 31:30, NLT).

"You will keep in perfect peace all who trust in you, whose thoughts are fixed on you!" (Isaiah 26:3, NLT).

_____

_____

_____

_____

_____

_____

_____

_____

_____

_____

_____

_____

_____

_____

_____

_____

_____

_____

_____

Humor Meets Praise

During my surgery and hospital stay, my husband made a valiant effort to keep our "prayer warriors" informed about my progress. But when I got home, I felt a responsibility to let them hear from me. I was doing well and wanted to communicate the grace of God that I had experienced. As I showered, I asked God how I could tell them how well I was doing, and how enormously grateful I was for their prayer support. I knew without a doubt that my strength was dependent on the prayers of others. God gave me the following to share with them:

THE 10 WORST THINGS ABOUT HAVING BREAST CANCER AND A MASTECTOMY

10. You are grounded longer than you'd like.

9. You run out of places to store the food friends bring for you and your family.

8. You miss all the good movies that premiere.

7. You can't hug your loved ones as tight as you'd like.

6. You can't pick up your grandchild and toss him in the air for a while.

5. You can't reach the glass or plate on the second shelf of the cabinet.

4. You can't open the refrigerator door when it's suctioned tight.

3. You can't eat the food people bring you because the antibiotics cause thrush in your mouth, and it burns until you get proper medication.

2. You can't go to church for a longer period than you would like.

And the number 1 worst thing about having a mastectomy?

Words are inadequate to express the gratitude you feel for all the expressions of love you receive in both tangible and intangible ways.

THE 10 BEST THINGS ABOUT HAVING
BREAST CANCER AND A MASTECTOMY

10. You get the best new recipes since the birth of your last child.

9. God has equipped people with skills and knowledge to treat cancer.

8. Saints of the world bathe you in prayer.

7. You experience God's peace in a supernatural, new way.

6. Everyone you talk to, tells you to eat.

5. Your children "rise up and called you blessed."

4. Your daughter becomes your nurse, with gentle and patient precision.

3. Your husband waits on you hand and foot.

2. God provides you with a new platform to declare His grace.

And the number 1 best thing about having a mastectomy?

You learn to depend on God and His sovereignty and are grateful for the opportunity, no matter the circumstance.

Your lists may vary, but I'm sure you too can find things to laugh and rejoice about.;-)

Journal

"To whom will you compare me? Who is my equal?' asks the Holy One. Look up into the heavens. Who created all the stars? He brings them out one after another, calling each by its name. And he counts them to see that none are lost or have strayed away. O Israel [add your name], how can you say the LORD does not see your troubles? How can you say God refuses to hear your case? Have you never heard or understood? Don't you know that the LORD is the everlasting God, the Creator of all the earth? He never grows faint or weary. No one can measure the depths of his understanding. He gives power to those who are tired and worn out; he offers strength to the weak. Even youths will become exhausted, and young men will give up. But those who wait on the LORD will find new strength. They will fly high on wings like eagles. They will run and not grow weary" (Isaiah 40:25–31, NLT).

_____

_____

_____

_____

_____

_____

_____

_____

_____

_____

_____

_____

_____

Total Surrender

One morning I was up early with the Lord, and I began to wonder about when Christ had "sweat blood" as He faced crucifixion for the sins of mankind. What, specifically, had He dreaded most? Now there is a thought! Was it dying and taking on the sin of all humanity? Was it the battle with Satan? Was it the separation from God the Father? What overwhelmed Him the most? Christ knew that He had come to earth for this very purpose, yet He went before the Father, in the Garden of Gethsemane, one last time to say,

> *"My Father! If it is possible, let this cup of suffering be taken away from me. Yet I want your will, not mine"* (Matthew 26:39, *NLT*).

I jumped from that thought to my own battle. What did I dread the most as I faced cancer and the prescribed treatment? Was it the mastectomy? Was it losing my hair? Was it the nausea? Was it the total unknown future that lay ahead? Was it that God may be using cancer to end my mortal life? What I came to realize was that I had to, once again, surrender my will to that of the Father. I dreaded being asked to surrender totally to Him in faith, one more time.

In *Simply Jesus (p. 79-80)*, Dr. Joseph Stowell refers to this issue, stating, "Being conformed to His death means full surrender to our Father's will—regardless. No excuses. No escape clauses. No negotiation. . . Jesus would not be deterred. He could have called twelve legions of angels, exercising His rights and power. . . ." Dr. Stowell goes on to recount how Christ not only surrendered, but He persevered in total obedience. He set "the pattern for us to follow in our lives if we are to know Jesus. An undaunted and nonnegotiable loyalty to Jesus—regardless of the cost—is the key to deepening, intimate fellowship with Him." Long ago, during a difficult time of personal spiritual growth, I ultimately discovered that I would rather surrender in total dismay and be broken in the center of God's perfect will, than live in ignorant peace in the center of my own will. Once again, I was reminded that being a living sacrifice was a difficult job. I had to stay put and wait on God. I was faced with **total surrender**.

It really didn't matter if my hair fell out or my mouth was full of sores. What about nausea and diarrhea, or delays in treatment due to low counts? There are many difficult situations that we face in a life dedicated to glorifying Christ. Maybe the most difficult is yielding our lives to His glory in total surrender.

Journal

"This suffering is all part of what God has called you to. Christ, who suffered for you, is your example. Follow in his steps. He never sinned, and he never deceived anyone. He did not retaliate when he was insulted. When he suffered, he did not threaten to get even. He left his case in the hands of God, who always judges fairly. He personally carried away our sins in his own body on the cross so we can be dead to sin and live for what is right" (1 Peter 2:21–24, NLT).

Total surrender means being able to stand as Paul did and proclaim:

"For to me, to live is Christ, and to die is gain" (Philippians 1:21, NKJV).

Expectations

Following surgery, I began to examine my expectations, particularly about my body and my future. What could the physicians do, and what would be impossible?

It is important to look at expectations, because unfulfilled expectations can lead to huge disappointments. It is critical to have realistic expectations regarding surgery and treatment. Doctors can surgically replace a removed breast. They can implement procedures to attack cancer cells. They can give hope where fear once lived. They can prescribe tests and scans to look deeper into the body that, in times past, were not even thought possible.

What are your expectations? Do you realize you have pre-existing expectations that you are not even aware of? Do you expect to be scar-free following your surgery? Will you choose a lumpectomy, when a mastectomy would be a wiser choice, because you are afraid to lose your breast? Will the presence of a scar cause you to look away from your body in horror? Do you see a scar as being disfigured? Is your sexuality and femininity tied to your breast? Will grief and loss consume you? These are all very valid concerns. You will need to examine your own fears and expectations.

I bring up expectations because if they are ignored, disappointment and depression can set in. Being realistic with your options is very helpful. No doctor can give you a 100% guarantee of a cure once you are diagnosed with invasive or inflammatory breast cancer. You will not be scar-free if you choose a mastectomy. In some cases, a lumpectomy can leave the area very disfigured because of the amount of tissue that must be removed. If a single mastectomy is done, the two breasts may never look exactly the same. The physicians can do amazing work in reconstruction, but your expectations must be realistic.

Let me caution you, once again, to go to both your journal and the Word of God. Let His presence comfort you and bring you security. If you feel the cloud of depression setting in, talk to your physician. Look to a grief counselor. Consider all your options.

Expectations

Don't sit in despair. You need your emotional strength, as well as, your spiritual and physical strength.

Journal

"My son, keep sound wisdom and discretion; let them not escape from your sight, and they will be life for your soul and adornment for your neck. Then you will walk on your way securely and your foot will not stumble. If you sit down, you will not be afraid; when you lie down, your sleep will be sweet. Do not be afraid of sudden panic,... for the LORD *will be your confidence and will keep your foot from being caught"* (Proverbs 3:21–26, RSV).

Yuck! Chemo

For some, chemotherapy comes before the surgery and for others radiation. For me, it followed six weeks after the surgery. I met a new doctor and learned the words for the treatment I was facing. I was probably as interested in the side effects of the treatment as the treatment itself. My doctor friend had told me to ask about the side effects and weigh the treatment against the potential consequences. I knew the treatment involved putting toxic poisons into my body using a needle (some necessitate a port, requiring day surgery). Beyond that, I knew I'd probably lose my hair, fight nausea, maybe have brittle fingernails, and so on. These were the consequences I expected. Later I learned to ask about possible heart damage and the possibility of leukemia.

The medications themselves were just plain nasty, but necessary. Things I loved to eat no longer tasted good; my body became lethargic because all my healthy antibodies were zapped along with the unhealthy cancer cells. For me, thrush became an issue and caused miserable sores in my mouth (it was easily treated). I feared nausea, and maybe most of all, I feared losing my hair. Fortunately, the oncologist was very concerned about my wellbeing and made every effort to prevent the nausea. This was accomplished with a cocktail of anti-nausea medications given before and after the chemo.

I learned that before they are willing to give the chemo, they must do blood tests to make sure all "the numbers" are high enough for the body to sustain the treatment. Red and white cells, along with platelets, must be at a certain level or the body would be too weak to endure the assault of the treatment.

The "infusion lab," where nurses administer the treatment prescribed by the doctor, has numerous chairs for a variety of people receiving chemo. Some are there, as I was, for a short period of only four cycles (one every three weeks). Others are there daily, weekly, or monthly. It's easy to become a family with these strangers because they understand the fear and anxiety that accompany you each time you walk through that door. This was one place it was really safe to talk about fear. On my second visit I saw a woman about my age who was absolutely trembling with fear. I had already lost my hair, and it was quite apparent that I was ahead of her in treatment. The Lord just moved me to go speak with her and hold her hand while she waited for the nurse to come to her. I'm sure I received more of a blessing than she did just by saying to her, "You look really scared." She replied that she was petrified, and I could comfort her by saying, "That's okay, it's a scary place." This time I got to be "Jesus in skin" to someone else. I really learned to love touching others in the lab. Experiencing God's peace   and   sharing it with others brought great comfort to me.

Journal

"You are the light of the world—like a city on a mountain, glowing in the night for all to see. Don't hide your light under a basket! Instead, put it on a stand and let it shine for all. In the same way, let your good deeds shine out for all to see, so that everyone will praise your heavenly Father" (Matthew 5:14–16, NLT).

Tunnel Vision

Your journey through surgery, radiation, and chemotherapy may go smoothly - just as scheduled, one right after the other. When it does, rejoice with praise and thanksgiving. The completion of this segment of the pilgrimage is a time for celebration.

Others have unpredictable complications, bringing on the dark cloud of fear and frustration. From the very beginning, we are looking to the end. We keep track of each segment: first treatment down, only seven to go; radiation is over, now the surgery is scheduled; day ten following chemo and energy is beginning to return; expanders are full, time for the "real thing." There are numerous steps that pass beneath our feet on the sometimes steep, always rocky and often fickle path. Of one thing we are confident, with each step forward, we are one step closer to the end. We are focused on the end of the tunnel. We develop tunnel vision. We plod forward, one arduous step after another, clutching our hopes and fears. Then we begin to see the "light at the end of the tunnel." Our expectations take over, and our minds begin to race to the light!

Then, as if mysteriously out of nowhere, something totally unexpected happens. An infection develops, the counts are too low, there is an emergency appendectomy, or one of the team of doctors resigns to take a new position. The circumstances are countless, but the consequences are generally the same -- an emotional roller coaster ride. Yet again we are reminded that nowhere, at any time, are we in control of that "yet to be known" design for our lives. Our precious Lord continues to orchestrate a plan specific for our personal needs. In so doing He reminds us, not so subtly, that we are to rely totally on His strength and His timing. Just in calling Him "Lord" all things are put into perspective.

If you are one of the many who experience what feels like a devastating blow to your progress, step back, call your trusted and steadfast friend and "vent" your disappointment and frustrations. At first you may not be able to stop and pray about it because you cannot fathom getting side-tracked and delayed. This really cannot be happening! When your emotional tidal wave has calmed, kneel before your Savior, look Him straight in the eye, and feel his gentle touch on your soul. Pour yourself out into His presence. He will embrace your tormented fear and encourage your fractured spirit.

Could it be that you are experiencing doubt as the disciples did in Matthew 8? First, we read that the disciples watched as Christ healed a man of leprosy. N6ext, He tells a Roman officer that his faith alone has caused his servant to be healed. Immediately following the healing, we see Christ is in Peter's mother-in-law's home. She has a high fever, and just His touch cures her. On and on it goes. The disciples watched with privileged intimacy as people came to Christ for His gentle touch, and their faith touched His heart.

We don't want to see ourselves filled with doubt, as the disciples were, but here we sit with burning tears of fear and anxiety flowing down faith-battered cheeks. We are so terribly, terribly tired of the battle with the ever-present onerous enemy. We want desperately to close the curtain on this chapter of our life - on this unwelcome intruder. But the Lord says "not yet". No, we are forced to pry open the vault of our mind and our emotions and do our housekeeping.

Once again, but never too often, we are reminded of the steadfast love of our Heavenly Father, and of the length and breadth that our Lord went to in order to allow us the privilege of relationship with Him. We also have the power of the indwelling Holy Spirit from which to draw.

May the battles of your journey be silenced by your willingness to do as Abraham did, when God commanded him to take his only son Isaac up Mount Moriah to offer him as a burnt offering. Upon his arrival, Abraham had Isaac carry wood for the altar. When Isaac questioned his father about the sacrifice needed, Abraham quickly responded that God would provide a lamb. Because of his faith, Abraham was counted righteous.

You and I worship the same immutable God. He is forever steadfast; never changing. He will not be more perfect tomorrow, more loving next year, or more just at the pearly gate. He is 100% perfect; 100% love; 100% just. This is how He always has been, even before time began, and will be into eternity. It is the Alpha and Omega that we have access to. Don't waste your tears and fears. You have sought out the best medical team and look to them to do all that is possible with the resources that are available to them. Shouldn't you do the same with your Spiritual team?

Journal

"My help comes from the Lord, who made the heavens and the earth! He will not let you stumble and fall; the one who watches over you will not sleep. Indeed, he who watches over Israel never tires and never sleeps. The Lord himself watches over you! The Lord stands beside you as your protective shade.... The Lord keeps watch over you as you come and go, both now and forever." (Psalm 121:2-5, 8 NLT)

"Why are you afraid? You have so little faith!" Then he stood up and rebuked the wind and waves and suddenly all was calm. The disciples just sat there in awe. "Who is this?" they asked themselves." (Matthew 8:26-27 NLT)

"I have fought a good fight, I have finished the race, and I have remained faithful. And now the prize awaits me - the crown of the righteousness that the Lord, the righteous Judge, will give me on that great day of his return. And the prize is not just for me but for all who eagerly look forward to his glorious return." (2 Timothy 4:7-8 NLT)

_____

_____

_____

_____

_____

_____

_____

_____

_____

Pity Party

Two and a half weeks after my first chemotherapy, I was on vacation doing the recovery thing. The weather was so refreshing, and the scenery stood as a testimony to the majesty of our heavenly Father. The aspen leaves shimmered, reflecting shades of gold and amber. The mountains climbed to the heavens, and the hummingbirds worked feverishly feeding themselves and pollinating the numerous flowers planted around the area. And to confirm His magnificence, God painted a double rainbow across the sky for us following a refreshing afternoon thunderstorm. We all just bathed in our Creator's desire to share with us the awesomeness of His glory.

The latter part of the week, I began to see my newly short (really short!) hair coming out in the tub, on my clothes, in my hands—just everywhere. This was not a good thing. It was not a surprise, but what had been anticipated was now actually happening. I was doing some shopping and I began to sink into grief. He was really moving in too close to my pride and vanity. I felt as though I might cry, but then I began to think of my Lord and Savior, stripped naked, bleeding from the flogging of the Roman solders, walking through the streets of Jerusalem carrying a cross on my behalf. I began to see His humility and sacrifice for me.

I reflected on an Amy Carmichael devotional I had read earlier in the week about "touching the hem of His garment as He passed by." I had prayed that He would pass by me and that I would have the faith to rejoice simply by "touching the hem of His garment." Well, I guess this was my opportunity to touch that hem, and I failed miserably. I called my husband and said that I was going to buy some hats because I thought my hair would fall out before I got back to Texas. After getting back to our condo, I pretty much picked a fight with my husband as he tried to show me compassion. I didn't want compassion - I wanted a pity party!

The next day was much better. First, I confessed that I had not been consolable and asked for forgiveness. Then I focused on my hair. I discovered that if you use enough gel you can kind of "glue" your hair to your scalp, at least, temporarily. So, for the next two days, I did just that. As long as I didn't touch it, I was okay. Almost immediately upon our return home, I went to the beauty shop and asked a young woman to shave my head. I told her I couldn't bear to watch, so she turned the chair so that I couldn't see either mirror from front or back. I sat there and prayed as she "buzzed" my scalp, "God, don't let me cry here." I had never met this young woman before, but she shared with me that she had done this numerous times. She was very tender and compassionate. It really was an amazing experience. I genuinely dreaded turning to the mirror, especially in front of other people. I was so afraid I would burst into tears and wash away my testimony to God's glory and sufficiency. I had become so bound up in fear of how I would look and how people would respond to me. The fear melted away as she turned me to face the mirror.

I continued to praise God for the family that is knit together by the blood of the Lamb. And, I relied on their prayers and His Word to walk through the opportunity God gave me. (I dread the day when   I   am strong and relying on my own sufficiency again.)

Journal

"My grace is sufficient for you, for my power is made perfect in weakness.' I will all the more gladly boast of my weaknesses, that the power of Christ may rest upon me" (2 Corinthians 12:9, NLT).

_____

_____

_____

_____

_____

_____

_____

_____

_____

_____

_____

_____

_____

_____

_____

_____

_____

_____

_____

Intimacy with the Lord

There were moments sprinkled about my recovery, when I felt such intimacy with God that I was overwhelmed with His presence and by the fact that His perfect love had found me. One day, in particular, I sat alone with His Word thinking about a sinus infection that I feared would grip me and prolong my treatment. I had already faced one bout with "thrush" and anticipated another attack at any moment. Poor me!

I looked out the window, as I convalesced, and began to take in the magnificence of His creation. The sun crept over the top of the mountain. The skies were washed in a clear transparent powder blue, and the leaves on the aspen trees glistened with the reflection of the light from the sun. The daisies stood tall as if they were reaching to touch the glory of Christ. I saw birds take flight seeking their provisions as He had promised.

I realized, for one short moment, I was allowed to see the majesty of God clearly in everything that lived outside the four walls that surrounded me.

Instantly, the spell was broken, and I was back in my room confronted with the total inadequacy of man's ability to build anything compared to God's capacity to create. I was grateful for the "creature comforts" that surround my life, but even more, I was thankful for a moment's revelation of God's splendor and grandeur. This time I didn't miss it! God's breath had fallen gently on my soul, and I was drenched in the glory of his presence.

Take time to reflect and look around your world during your convalescence. Identify God's presence. He is there--right there. He desires to be seen and praised in all circumstances. You will be forever blessed for your effort.

Journal

"Yours, O LORD, is the greatness, the power, the glory, the victory, and the majesty. Everything in the heavens and on earth is yours, O LORD, and this is your kingdom. We adore you as the one who is over all things. Riches and honor come from you alone, for you rule over everything. Power and might are in your hand, and it is at your discretion that people are made great and given strength. O our God, we thank you and praise your glorious name!" (1 Chronicles 29:11–13, NLT).

"Shout with joy to the LORD, O earth! Worship the LORD with gladness. Come before him, singing with joy. Acknowledge that the LORD is God! He made us, and we are his. We are his people, the sheep of his pasture. Enter his gates with thanksgiving; go into his courts with praise. Give thanks to him and bless his name. For the LORD is good. His unfailing love continues forever, and his faithfulness continues to each generation" (Psalm 100:1–5, NLT).

_____

_____

_____

_____

_____

_____

_____

_____

_____

_____

_____

What Does Trust Look Like?

Are Trust and Faith Interchangeable?

What does it look like to trust Christ? How does anyone get from verbalizing trust to actually experiencing trust? God's Word tells us a lot about trust, and we desire with all that we are to walk by faith. We recognize that faith in the sacrificial blood of Christ is our only hope. We can even display trust, fairly well, when our stomachs are full, our health is strong, and our loved ones are fulfilling our dreams for them. When everything is going our way, we can testify to the goodness and generosity of God.

When my children chose to trust Christ as their Savior, I was one proud parent. I had obviously done my job well and accomplished my goal! When my husband got a promotion at work, I relished in the rewards he received for his hard work. When I graduated with honors after going back to college in my forties, my sense of self-esteem was elevated to new heights. With each new accomplishment, I was able to give God the glory for all He had done for me and my family. This was particularly true of those things that made me look like such a good mother, wife, and student. Hadn't I earned the accomplishment with my own hard work, determination, and many hours on my knees? Now I was equipped to tell others how to succeed just as I had done.

Then there was the day my husband was unjustly removed from a position of authority; there were the nights I sat by my teenage twins' sides and listened to their desire to die; I watched as my gifted children chose to flunk classes instead of study. My personal esteem was pulverized. Where was God now? Hadn't I taught my children Scripture from the time they could recite their ABC's? Why would God turn His back on me? Hadn't I been obedient?

Could I trust my God to protect my children from their own self-loathing? I didn't think I could. What I soon learned was that I really had no other choice. Only my trust in God's Word and my prayer for their protection could bring me peace of mind. As my twins were ripped from my hands by their own willfulness, I fell on my face in total and utter failure, and came to a point of complete desperation. I could no longer control their choices or behavior. I was forced to look to God to do the work He had to do to make them the adults He (and I) wanted them to be. There was no knot to tie at the end my rope--only a free fall. I didn't know what would happen next, and I was terribly uncomfortable being out of control.

Next, there was the opportunity to walk by faith and trust in God's Word. After several years of yielding my children to God, and weeping day and night at the sense of loss I felt because they did not become the adults I had dreamed of, I discovered that God was busy with these young men. He hadn't abandoned me. He simply chose to bring them to Himself down a path I had not seen. I watched my adult children transformed into radiant Christians who embraced their faith with more vigor and passion than I could have anticipated. With this knowledge, it wasn't difficult for me to trust God with my cancer. Experiencing God's steadfast refuge with my sons brought me confidence with my journey through life with cancer. I was not in uncharted waters. He prepared a navigational chart for my life even before my lungs took breath.

Is there anyone out there who really believes they can control their cancer? We can try, and we manage to do some good things. But control? No. When we are able to relinquish our "illusion" of control to God, He is able to do far more with our lives than when we are busy "directing traffic". That trust is translated into peace that affects all those we come in contact with. Trust becomes something that is visible, almost tangible—seen in our smile, our prayers, our conversation, our sickness, our losses or gains, our sorrow, and our testimony. Yes, trust and faith are interchangeable. They overlap and they change lives. When you find that place of total trust, all of the surgery, treatment, and unknown future become simply a journey to walk with the Lord.

Journal

"But blessed are those who trust in the LORD and have made the LORD their hope and confidence. They are like trees planted along a riverbank, with roots that reach deep into the water. Such trees are not bothered by the heat or worried by long months of drought. Their leaves stay green, and they go right on producing delicious fruit" (Jeremiah 17:7–8, emphasis added, NLT).

"For when your faith is tested, your endurance has a chance to grow. So let it grow, for when your endurance is fully developed, you will be strong in character and ready for anything" (James 1:3–4, NLT).

"Now faith is the substance of things hoped for, the evidence of things not seen. . . . But without faith it is impossible to please Him, for he who comes to God must believe that He is, and that He is a rewarder of those who diligently seek Him" (Hebrews 11:1, 6, NKJV).

_____

_____

_____

_____

_____

_____

_____

_____

_____

_____

_____

_____

Now That It's Over,
I Want a Lifetime Guarantee!

Yes, I want a guarantee! I've done the cancer thing. I've done surgery, chemotherapy, radiation, reconstruction, and through most of that I was bald! I've thrown up, I've lost weight and gained weight (not liking either one), and at times my mouth was filled with sores. I felt like Job. It's not fair to have to go through all that and not get a written guarantee that I won't be back in here next year or ten years from now. I want to know that I'll see my children and grandchildren grow up. I want to watch them hunt Easter eggs. I want to tell them about Jesus. I want to go on hikes and share the majesty of God's creation. I don't want to have to see a doctor every three months, every six months, or at all. I've seen all the doctors I ever want to see; just getting on the elevator makes my stomach flutter. Don't I deserve time off? Haven't my family and I endured enough for a lifetime? Well, to put it concisely, in a word "NO!"

I do have a guarantee. It's found in Hebrews 9:27–28 -- I will die. Scripture tells us only Enoch and Elijah escaped this world without dying (Enoch in Genesis 5:18ff. and Hebrews 11:5; Elijah in 2 Kings 2:11–12). During my chemotherapy, my 93-year-old Dad passed away. I could rejoice in his passing because he knew Jesus as his personal Savior. He had lived a very long and sometimes difficult life. Yet, he gave me a heritage of integrity, faith, and hope. As I watched his body wither away, I was keenly aware that there was a much better place for him. Releasing him was one of the easiest difficult things I have ever done.

Also, during the last chemo treatment, my second grandson was born. On the very day! Needless to say, I couldn't be there, but in a very short period of time I was allowed to see life come full circle. I rejoiced in both the birthing and burying of these very precious loved ones. Just as my grandson had no say in when he would enter this world, neither did my Dad have a say about his time of exit.

What we *do* have a say about, is how we choose to live and the impact and heritage we leave to those that follow. I believe the greatest tragedy would be wasting the opportunity that we are given.

Journal

"Teach me to do your will, for you are my God. May your gracious Spirit lead me forward on a firm footing. For the glory of your name, O LORD, save me. In your righteousness, bring me out of this distress" (Psalm 143:10–11, NLT).

"So teach us to number our days that we may get a heart of wisdom" (Psalm 90:12, RSV).

_____

_____

_____

_____

_____

_____

_____

_____

_____

_____

_____

_____

_____

_____

_____

_____

_____

_____

Sexuality, My Husband, and My Breast

If you are married, are you concerned about your marriage or sexuality? How will your husband handle your surgery, reconstruction, and the demands for follow-up treatment? Do you and your husband have an intimate enough relationship that you can discuss the mastectomy and reconstruction openly without feelings of rejection? This experience is also happening to your husband - just as it is happening to you. We are reminded both in the Old and New Testament:

> *"'For this reason a man shall leave his father and mother and be joined to his wife, and the two shall become one flesh,'...they are no longer two but one flesh. Therefore what God has joined together, let not man separate" (Matthew 19:5-6; see Genesis 2:24; NKJV).*

Your husband may be filled with fear of his own. He doesn't know about mammograms and lumpectomies. He's probably heard of mastectomy and breast cancer, but it is doubtful that he has a friend to talk to, or resources that are common to us. Most of us know at least one person who has walked this road. Maybe their husband would be a good resource for your husband. Certainly he should be included in your doctor visits. He needs to be part of the decision-making process. He needs to hear the risk and consequences of treatment, as well as the chances of survival. He will soon learn that breast cancer can happen to men, as well. He needs to be with you to hear the second opinions. You need to make him part of your team. He will walk every step of the way with you and it is most likely that he is the least equipped of the group.

The Lord desires that, as He reveals Himself, you and your husband will grow stronger together through this trial. I was saddened to hear from my surgical oncologist that too many husbands walk out because they can't handle watching their wife in such pain. What a tragedy! First, she is confronted with the battle of cancer, and then with being abandoned. If you find yourself in this situation, you and your spouse need to find a counselor immediately! This issue must be addressed and resolved. A very helpful internet chat room, for cancer patients and family members, can be found at www.breastcancer.org/support.html. You can ask your questions anonymously and gather different perspectives. I'm sorry to say that I didn't find a "faith-based" web site for cancer patients, but there certainly may be one out there.

To aid you and your husband, I have asked my husband to contribute his thoughts. I know you and your husband will find them comforting.

Journal

"Trust in the LORD with all your heart; do not depend on your own understanding. Seek his will in all you do, and he will direct your paths" (Proverbs 3:5–6, NLT).

"I cried out, 'I'm slipping!' and your unfailing love, O LORD, supported me. When doubts filled my mind, your comfort gave me renewed hope and cheer" (Psalm 94:18, NLT).

_____

_____

_____

_____

_____

_____

_____

_____

_____

_____

_____

_____

_____

_____

_____

_____

_____

Keeping an Eternal Perspective

When one of my prayer warriors wrote to me that she was praying that I would keep an eternal perspective, I was brought to my knees. I was grateful that she had prayed for me in such a way, and to be reminded of that need. Sometimes it was difficult to stay focused on the eternal because I was so busy taking care of the immediate: a blood test here, a doctor appointment there. Did I remember to renew my prescription? Were there two scans scheduled today, or one? And the regular stuff—the laundry, meals, quiet time, and so on. I would love to have a manicure or a massage. Can you believe I need a haircut? The demands for the urgent can overwhelm the demand for the important.

Has your bout with cancer caused you to lose your eternal perspective? Do your thoughts dwell on what you may miss if your treatment is not successful? As I consider the number of years that are allotted to me (according to Psalm 90:12), I am reminded that whether it be 25, 56, or 93 (as given to my Dad) my life is but a vapor. Because of the cancer, I have been made keenly aware of my mortality. God's Word counsels me to make the most of the time and opportunities given me. This counsel consumes my thoughts and draws me back to His Word. My heart desires to know, right now, what God has in store for me tomorrow. I will not beg for 20 more years of quantity time, but pray that whatever time is left will be quality. More than ever, I desire to make my time and efforts count for eternity. I do not want to stand before Jesus on judgment day and place my works at His feet only to see them go up in flames. My time wishing this had never happened, or wondering how many more Christmases I'll be allowed, drains me of God's perspective. This may be the most significant opportunity I ever have to glorify my Savior. Please, Lord, don't let me fail! I know I have today. Be glorified!

When I acquire an eternal perspective, I see that my days are numbered and I praise God for His Son, my Savior, and that I will spend eternity in heaven.

Journal

"Your Word is a lamp to my feet and a light for my path" (Psalm 119:105, NLT).

"Come now, you who say, 'Today or tomorrow we will go to such and such a city, spend a year there, buy and sell, and make a profit'; whereas you do not know what will happen tomorrow. For what is your life? It is even a vapor that appears for a little time and then vanishes away" (James 4:13–14, NKJV).

"Now anyone who builds on that foundation may use gold, silver, jewels, wood, hay, or straw. But there is going to come a time of testing at the judgment day to see what kind of work each builder has done. Everyone's work will be put through the fire to see whether or not it keeps its value. If the work survives the fire, that builder will receive a reward. But if the work is burned up, the builder will suffer great loss. The builders themselves will be saved, but like someone escaping through a wall of flames" (1 Corinthians 3:12–15, NLT).

"Behold, I tell you a mystery: We shall not all sleep, but we shall all be changed—in a moment, in the twinkling of an eye, at the last trumpet. For the trumpet will sound, and the dead will be raised incorruptible, and we shall be changed. For this corruptible must put on incorruption, and this mortal must put on immortality. So when this corruptible has put on incorruption, and this mortal has put on immortality, then shall be brought to pass the saying that is written: 'Death is swallowed up in victory'" (1 Corinthians 15:51–54, NKJV).

"Therefore you also be ready, for the Son of Man is coming at an hour you do not expect" (Luke 12:40, NKJV).

_____

_____

_____

_____

Journal

A few words for

Your husband

from

My husband . . .

This Just Can't Be Happening!

Why is it that really bad news only chooses to visit our household when I am out of town? I was in London when it chose to come knocking on our door this time.

Five little words are what I heard from my wife over the phone as she said, "Honey, I have breast cancer." Hearing those words was like being slugged in the gut by "Smokin' Joe Frazier." I couldn't even breathe, much less respond. Immediately, my mind began to race to possible escapes from this reality. Maybe I was asleep and this was merely a dream; no, more like a nightmare. Maybe it was a wrong number and the voice I heard really wasn't Sue's. No, indeed it was Sue, and I was wide-awake. Oh, Dear God, not my beloved, not her! This just can't be happening, but it was.

This just isn't fair. Why Sue, of all people? She loves the Lord, she serves the Lord, and she is a Bible Study Fellowship (BSF) class administrator. Sue serves in multiple capacities in our church. She does not deserve this. If God wants to punish one of us, it should be me, not her.

But bad things can and do happen to good people. We probably all remember the story of Job, but there is also the story of Joseph in Genesis chapter 37. He was the son of Jacob, but was sold into slavery by his brothers. One moment, Joseph was living the good life as the favorite son, the next he was a slave on his way to Egypt, sold out by his own flesh and blood. Of course, there was more to that story than a bad beginning. God had big plans for Joseph, beyond anything he could have dreamed. I can just imagine how many times Joseph asked the question, "Why is this horrible thing happening to me?" Often we are confused or taken aback by the way a journey begins for us, because we can't see what the future has in store. Unfortunately, what we can see in the "here and now" is not looking very good.

Finally, I began to say to myself, "I've got to gather my wits about me. I've got to be strong for her, to provide support and encouragement in one of her greatest moments of need. I can't let her see through to my inner self to discover that right now I'm *not* the tower of strength she needs. No, I'm scared to death, that's what I am."

Journal

Oh Dear God, Help Me. Please Help Me!

I can't even hold her or hug her, and tell her I am there for her, because I'm not there for her—I'm on the other side of the world.

I've had this feeling before. I remember when our twin sons were close to delivery, the doctor said, "Her blood pressure has skyrocketed on us and we have to take the boys right now before she goes into toxic shock!" He turned, and pretty much ran back into the operating room. Wait! Don't go yet! What do you mean skyrocketed? What is toxic shock? Oh man, this is bad isn't it? What a sickening feeling! My wife is in trouble, apparently in real danger, and I'm just standing there like the "village idiot". I don't have a clue as to what is going on, and I am completely unable to come to her rescue. I tell you, a husband is not supposed to be helpless like this, just standing there, impotent in the face of danger.

Now, once again, I am standing there paralyzed and unable to move, while a terrible enemy is besieging my wife, threatening her very life. I can't see this enemy, fight it, or defend her against it. Oh, Dear God, help me, please help me.

I don't know about you, but I don't like feeling completely helpless. Worse yet, having to admit that I don't just feel helpless, I am helpless. However, it seems that it in those same moments, I find myself turning to God and seeking Him for my source of strength; looking to the One who can rescue my beloved.

I remember that God doesn't move away from me, and it is with no small amount of shame that I recall the distance I sometimes put between us. It seems arrogant to ask for the God of the universe to make haste to come and help me. Yet, I recall the story of Lazarus, and remember that Mary and Martha were in a hurry for Christ to come to the aid of Lazarus.

Journal

"A man named Lazarus was sick. He lived in Bethany with his sisters, Mary and Martha. This is the Mary who poured the expensive perfume on the Lord's feet and wiped them with her hair. Her brother, Lazarus, was sick. So the two sisters sent a message to Jesus telling him, "Lord, the one you love is very sick" (John 11:1–3, NKJV)

_____

_____

_____

_____

_____

_____

_____

_____

_____

_____

_____

_____

_____

_____

_____

_____

_____

_____

_____

_____

You Have to Be There for Her, No Matter What!

What am I doing? I'm crying out to God to help <u>me</u>? I'm not the one who needs help right now. Help Sue, please protect her, give her comfort and peace, and keep her in the shadow of Your wings. Guide the hands of the surgeons and all who assist in the procedures to come.

Toxic shock sounded bad, but cancer is just the worst. I mean, what could be worse than cancer? The "C" word just shakes you to the very core. Visions of the grim reaper begin to form in the shadows of your mind. Suddenly, you are face to face with your own mortality. I've got to pull myself together. I need a plan. What do I do next? Well, for one thing, I have to rearrange my priorities. I've got to be there for Sue; I've got to come alongside her in this battle. I've got to stand tall and be a pillar of strength. Make no mistake about it, though, I must get on my knees to find that strength. My greatest source of strength will come from above, not from within.

It seems to me that God's ways are sometimes strange compared to man's. Why is it that the greatest source of strength comes from a reservoir you can only approach from a position of humbleness and humility? A warrior would tell you that a man on his knees, head bowed and eyes closed, is the picture of a defeated man. God's Word tells us that a prayer warrior will rise and stand tall in the face of the enemy. When a man empties himself of his own power, and fills that emptied space with power from God, he is a man thoroughly equipped for the battlefield.

Husbands, go to your knees often, and as you rise, remember the lady you married. You are her lover, her companion, her friend, and her comforter. You vowed before man and God to love her till death do you part. Well sir, now is your time—more than ever—to be there for her. Don't falter; don't fail her— not now. I doubt she will ever need you more than she needs you right now. Cry out to God for the strength and courage you **both** will need for such a journey. No matter how difficult, no matter how tiring, <u>stay the course</u>.

Journal

Draw strength from what Paul wrote to Timothy.

"I have fought the good fight, I have finished the course, I have kept the faith." *(2 Timothy 4:7, NASB)*

_____

_____

_____

_____

_____

_____

_____

_____

_____

_____

_____

_____

_____

_____

_____

_____

_____

_____

_____

_____

Remember Your Vows

"I Do"

A covenant was made so long ago. I had no idea what I was doing or heading into. Looking back, I realize I simply had no understanding of the journey that lay before us.

"I Do"

Of course, I was only thinking of how good it was and how much better it was going to be. The "worse" part . . . well that wouldn't be happening to us After all, we were good-looking, intelligent, strong, young, and on our way. But life is chock-full of opposites; it must be some metaphysical balancing thing. There is:

Light *and* Dark

Good *and* Evil

Happy *and* Sad

Rich *and* Poor

And yes there is also . . .

For **Better** *or* **Worse**?

"Worse", for us, were things like toxic shock and raising twin boys, who redefined the term "strong willed." "Worse" was our daughter going through multiple surgeries for the removal of a large precancerous growth located on the crown of her head. And now we face breast cancer? I don't know what form "worse" will take in your lives, but it will show up in one form or another. This may be less for some and more for others. But it seems that if you live long enough, it is inevitable.

"I Do"

But why **this** sickness? Why Sue? And the response that comes back is, why not? I know that it is "appointed once unto every man to die", and that we don't get a say in how many days we are allotted. We just get to live them out. We are all familiar with the expression "that our days upon this earth are numbered". Well, if this is it for Sue, then I'm telling you I don't like Sue's "number" one bit! Oh man, what am I saying? I sure hope the Lord knows I didn't really mean to say that. Sometimes, I let my emotions drive my tongue ahead of my mind, and I just blurt out some of the dumbest things, instead of taking the time to think about what I'm going to say. I'm sorry to have to be the one to tell you, but, husbands, you are in for a lot of those times during this journey. It is just an emotional time, and most of us are more accustomed to curbing our emotions, than having them run amuck on us.

In times like these, I remember that others have gone through dark times as well. I believe some of Winston Churchill's finest hours as a statesman were during England's darkest hours of World War II. He didn't desire or ask for the war, but he determined to see it through, *and so must you* during your own war.

Journal

"But the Lord Jesus Christ has shown me that my days on earth are numbered and I am soon to die." (2 Peter 1:14, NLT).

Love and Devotion

I don't doubt for a moment that Sue will see this through; not in weakness, not in trembling fear, but meeting it head on, knowing in Whom she trusts. One day she said to me, "Doug, don't be greatly troubled by this, for God is sovereign. To live in Christ is fulfilling, and to die in Christ is gain. It's not really an ending, but rather a new and glorious beginning."

Where does she get such strength? There I go again with the stupid questions. Of course, I know the source. Even so, I marvel at her. She really doesn't need my strength, for she is strengthened from a far greater power. No, what she needs from me is simply my love and total devotion to her. I must love her throughout this dark and difficult chapter of our lives together.

In hindsight, through this frightening journey, I learned to express my love to Sue more meaningfully than ever before. I am convinced that your greatest responsibility, as well as your greatest privilege, will be to demonstrate over and over again the true act of devotion to your wife as she battles with this unseen enemy.

Oh man, here come those tears again; some hero I am. This crying thing will most likely occur with you as well, fellow husbands, often when you least expect it. Don't be concerned about it, just wipe the tears away and keep going.

I know I should not, but I keep asking myself "Why?" Of course, it is the God of Abraham that I should be asking "Why?" As I recall, I wasn't there when God created the universe, placed the stars in the heavens, and breathed life into Adam. Who am I to question God's plans, His purposes, and His will for Sue's life while here on this earth? In my mind I accept this, but in my heart of hearts, I still struggle. No doubt about it, I need more time on my knees, and trust me, so will you.

Journal

"Yea, though I walk through the valley of the shadow of death, I will fear no evil, for thou art with me; thy rod and thy staff they comfort me" (Psalm 23:4, KJV).

_____

_____

_____

_____

_____

_____

_____

_____

_____

_____

_____

_____

_____

_____

_____

_____

_____

_____

God Answers Knee-Mail

This topic title is just the kind of thing that brings forth groans . . . loud, long drawn-out groans from Sue and my children. I can just hear them now saying, "Dad, you are so corny you should have been a Kansas farmer." And yet, God does answer the prayers of the saints. You may not receive the answer you desire. You might not know when you will hear from Him. And, for a time, you may not hear Him very clearly.

I imagine you are like me, in that you want an answer right now! Yes, right now is when I want to hear from God; right now, not tomorrow, and not someday soon, but right now!

"....Look it up for yourself, you will profit more from the knowledge you obtain than if I simply give you the answer you seek." We've nearly all had this spoken to us by one teacher or another in our early school days.

Alas, God doesn't always respond with one very clear answer to a specific question. He often works in mysterious ways, and frankly, sometimes not so mysterious; just not in the way we want. No doubt, He believes we would profit more from going through a difficult trial, than to be spared the test and miss the valuable lesson He planned for us to learn.

While on our knees, men, let's learn to ask better, more thoughtful questions for the things that equip us, not just for the end result we desire. Pray for God's healing power, yes, but also for wisdom, strength, courage, compassion, and understanding. Pray for His guiding hand in our lives, for His peace in these troubling times and, oh, for about a hundred other things.

Journal

"It is good for me that I have been afflicted; that I might learn thy statutes." (Psalm 119:71, KJV)

"Confess your faults one to another, and pray one for another, that ye may be healed. The effectual fervent prayer of a righteous man availeth much" (James 5:16, KJV).

_____

_____

_____

_____

_____

_____

_____

_____

_____

_____

_____

_____

_____

_____

_____

_____

_____

_____

_____

_____

Raise up an Army of Prayer Warriors

Surround yourself with God's people. Raise up an army of prayer warriors to pray on your behalf, lifting up your beloved to God. I'm not saying God won't hear the uttering of one voice in the crowd, but rather that there is power in prayer. When more are praying, more power is being generated. The Holy Spirit intercedes on our behalf, so let's keep Him really busy with the uttering of the saints.

I know what you are thinking: "I just don't want to burden our friends with our struggles." **Do not**, I repeat, **do not** think this way! A true Christian friend will be anxious to pray for you and your wife. Don't just engage a few of your closest friends. Reach out and build an entire army to pray on her behalf.

Keep them informed of her progress, good days and bad, so they will know how to pray. You will draw strength from them. You will be in awe of the power that comes from such an army as this.

I would consider it a privilege to be one of your prayer warriors. If you find you'd like to talk with a fellow sojourner who has been down this road you're on, please feel free to write me at sojourner@amplifier.com.

Journal

"And the Holy Spirit helps us in our distress. For we don't even know what we should pray for, nor how we should pray. But the Holy Spirit prays for us with groanings that cannot be expressed in words" (Romans 8:26, NLT).

"These things I have spoken unto you, that in me ye might have peace. In the world ye shall have tribulation: but be of good cheer; I have overcome the world. (John 16:33, KJV)

_____

_____

_____

_____

_____

_____

_____

_____

_____

_____

_____

_____

_____

_____

_____

Printed in the United States
65175LVS00006B/235-432